The Church Is PEOPLE
the BODY of CHRIST

"Just as each of us has one body with many members, and these members do not all have the same function, so in Christ we who are many forms in one body, and each member belongs to all the others. We have different gifts."

Romans 12:4-6 (NIV)

"Now the body is not made up of one part but of many. If the **foot** should say, 'Because I am not a hand, I do not belong to the body,' it would not for that reason cease to be part of the body.

"And if the **ear** should say, 'Because I am not an eye, I do not belong to the body,' it would not for that reason cease to be part of the body.

(continued)

God's Special Gifts For Me   3

"If the whole body were an **eye**, where would the sense of hearing be? If the whole body were an **ear**, where would the sense of smell be?

"But in fact God has arranged the parts in the body, every one of them, just as he wanted them to be...

"The **eye** can not say to the **hand**, 'I don't need you!' And the **head** can not say to the **feet**, 'I don't need you!'

"If one part suffers, every part suffers with it; if one part is honored, every part rejoices with it. Now you are the body of Christ, and each one of you is a part of it."

1 Corinthians 12:14-18, 21, 26, 27 (NIV)

Philip the Evangelist

Do you know what an evangelist is? The dictionary tells us that it is "someone who brings good news." Although there are many evangelists in the Bible, Philip is the only person who is called an evangelist (in Acts 21:8).

In Acts 8:27-40 Philip shared the Gospel with the Ethiopian eunuch and baptized him. Like Philip, an evangelist proclaims the saving message of the Gospel. Evangelists are usually talkative and likeable. They are interested in the things that are going on in other people's lives. Most of all, they are concerned with each person's relationship with Jesus and want to help them make a decision to follow Jesus all their lives.

John the Baptist the Prophet

John the Baptist was a prophet, a person who spent his days preaching God's Word and baptizing early Christians. John was a "voice crying out in the wilderness"— he warned everyone he saw to turn from their sin and repent, for the Kingdom of God was at hand.

Prophets have the ability to explain God's Word in a way that points out sin and other things that are wrong in people's lives. The messages they preach help people recognize their sin, correct their ways, and live as Christ commands.

God's Special Gifts For Me

Aquila & Priscilla the Teachers

In Acts 18:24-26 Apollos was teaching in the synagogue, but his message was out of date, not current. Aquila and Priscilla, being familiar with the ministry of the Holy Spirit, took Apollos aside and taught, updated, and explained to him the way of God more accurately.

Teachers love to study in order to understand and explain God's Word. They thrive on accuracy by making all the pieces of Scripture fit. Teachers love to share what they have learned through their writing and public speaking.

Barnabas the Exhorter

Acts 11:22-24 tells us that Barnabas was a good man who was filled with the Holy Ghost. He exhorted, or encouraged, people so that they would be faithful to the Lord. The name Barnabas actually means "son of encouragement."

Exhorters are very practical teachers. They encourage others by giving practical steps to help them resolve their problems. They like to teach messages on different topics instead of teaching straight from the Bible. They lift the spirits of people who are discouraged and keep them from "giving up."

Timothy the Shepherd

Many biblical scholars believe Timothy was the pastor of the church at Ephesus. Paul's letters to Timothy seemed to be those of a church elder to a new pastor on how to organize his church.

Shepherd is another word for pastor, but the gift of shepherding is not limited to the pastor. Some shepherds use their gift as small group leaders, Sunday school teachers, or day care workers. Shepherds like to lead, counsel, teach, care for, pray for and oversee groups of believers.

The Good Samaritan the Mercy Shower

In Acts 10:30-37, Jesus tells us the parable of the Samaritan who showed mercy to a stranger who had been robbed, beaten, and left by the side of the road. The Samaritan bandaged his wounds, took him to a hotel, and paid for someone to care for him.

Mercy showers have compassion for people who are less fortunate than others, those who are hurting or have physical problems. Mercy showers are good listeners. They comfort other people and share their sorrows and joys.

God's Special Gifts For Me

The Widow Who Gave All
the Giver

In the Gospel of Mark, 12:41-44, Jesus commended the widow who gave out of her poverty. Although her gift was two mites (less than one penny today) it was more valuable in God's eyes than the great amounts of money all the others gave out of their abundance. The widow had the gift of giving.

All Christians have the responsibility of giving to God's work, but some have the ability to give far beyond their tithe (a tithe is 10% of their income). God gave these people the gift of giving. Givers have the ability to make wise financial decisions. Some have the ability to make a lot of money. Givers like to share the things they have with others.

Dorcas the Server

Acts 8:36 tells a story of Dorcas, a lady who used her gift of service by sewing for the widows of the church. When Dorcas died, she was so greatly missed that Peter, being touched, raised her from the dead.

Peter had a gift also. He had been used mightily by God as a preacher and healer, even raising Dorcas from the dead. Peter's gifts seemed more important than Dorcas' little gift of service...but when Peter died, no one raised him from the dead.

Servers like to help others. They don't like the spotlight on themselves, but prefer to work behind the scenes. Servers are not kings, but king makers.

Moses the Leader

Moses is possibly the greatest leader mentioned in the Bible. He led millions of God's people out of bondage, out of Egypt and into the Promised Land.

God still uses men and women like Moses to lead His people today. He uses men and women like Billy Graham, your pastor, your Sunday school teacher — and people just like you! God may have gifted you to lead others.

Leaders tend to step in and take charge when no one else is leading or when people are confused. They dream big dreams for God. Leaders organize people and things, set goals and give direction. They want to "get the ball rolling." Leaders also care for people and want to help them succeed.

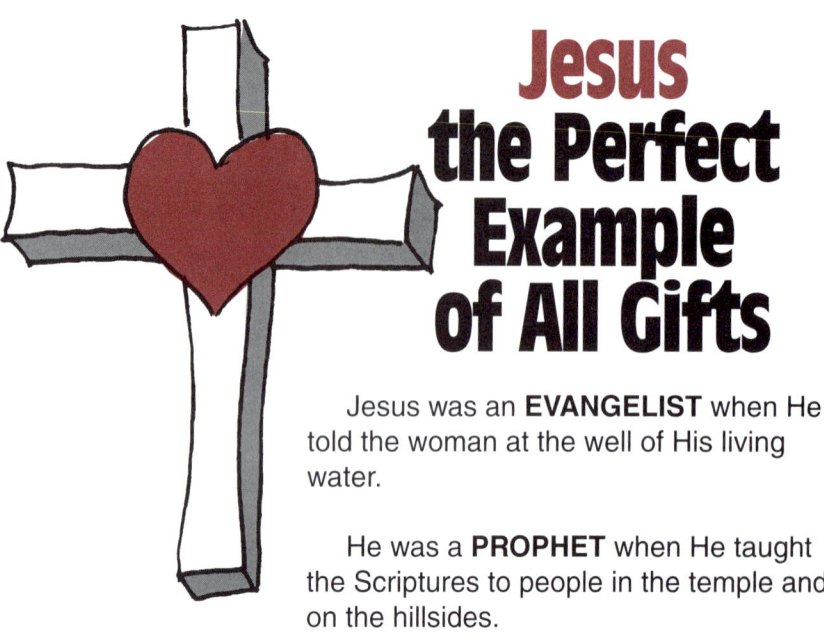

Jesus the Perfect Example of All Gifts

Jesus was an **EVANGELIST** when He told the woman at the well of His living water.

He was a **PROPHET** when He taught the Scriptures to people in the temple and on the hillsides.

He was a **TEACHER** when He preached the sermon on the mount.

He was an **EXHORTER** when He used parables to clearly explain His message.

He was a **SHEPHERD** when He led, taught and cared for the 12 disciples.

He was a **MERCY SHOWER** when He healed the sick and raised the dead.

He was a **SERVER** when He washed Peter's feet.

He was a **GIVER** when He gave His life by dying on the cross for our sins.

He will show that He is the greatest **LEADER** of all time when He returns as King of Kings and Lord of Lords.

What Best Describes You?
How I Add Up...

Instructions

Read the statements on the following three pages. Circle the number in the column that best describes how much you are like the statement. If you are "Usually" like the statement, circle the 2 at the end of the statement. If you are "Sometimes" like the statement, circle the 1. If you are "Not Very Often" like the statement, circle the 0. When you finish the first box, add up the numbers you have circled. Write the total in the "Add It Up" box. Go on until you have finished all nine boxes.

	Usually	Sometimes	Not Very Often

1

	Usually	Sometimes	Not Very Often
1. Whenever I can, I tell other people what Jesus did for us and that they can go to heaven.	2	1	0
2. God gives me boldness so I am not embarrassed to share my faith with people.	2	1	0
3. I pray for people who are not Christians.	2	1	0
4. I love to meet new people so I can share my faith with them.	2	1	0
5. I clearly understand God's message of salvation and can explain it to other people.	2	1	0
ADD IT UP			

2

	Usually	Sometimes	Not Very Often
1. I point out what is wrong and try to convince others to do right.	2	1	0
2. I enjoy speaking in front of other people.	2	1	0
3. I am able to explain things clearly and boldly to other people.	2	1	0
4. I think maybe God wants me to be a preacher some day.	2	1	0
5. I wish I could shout out to the whole world that they better get ready for Jesus to come back.	2	1	0
ADD IT UP			

God's Special Gifts For Me

	Usually	Sometimes	Not Very Often

3

1. I like to spend time studying. — 2 1 0
2. I would like to learn new things about what verses mean by looking in a Bible dictionary or encyclopedia. — 2 1 0
3. I think about what I want to say before I say it. — 2 1 0
4. I enjoy research. — 2 1 0
5. Details interest me. — 2 1 0

ADD IT UP

4

1. I'm not interested in a lot of facts unless it's something I can use in my life. — 2 1 0
2. When people near me don't understand something, I try to help them understand it. — 2 1 0
3. I give people "pep talks" and talk them into doing what they should do. — 2 1 0
4. When I grow close to God, I cannot help but share it with other people and help them grow too. — 2 1 0
5. I love to talk with people. — 2 1 0

ADD IT UP

5

1. Grown-ups would say I am more of a leader than a follower. — 2 1 0
2. In my classes, teams or group of friends, I notice how other people are doing. — 2 1 0
3. I like to be around people and care deeply for them. — 2 1 0
4. If someone were trying to lead anyone I know away from God's ways, I would try to stop them. — 2 1 0
5. I notice when people are missing from a group and check to see how they are. — 2 1 0

ADD IT UP

12 God's Special Gifts For Me

6

1. I notice other people's needs and do all I can to help. 2 1 0
2. I understand how other people feel and comfort them if needed. 2 1 0
3. I am not likely to yell at other people. 2 1 0
4. I am patient with other people. 2 1 0
5. When someone is being treated badly by other people, I stick up for him or her. 2 1 0

ADD IT UP

7

1. When I get money, I am most excited about how much I can give to God's work or what I can buy for someone else. 2 1 0
2. Whenever I hear of a financial need, I am happy to give whatever I have. 2 1 0
3. I give more than 10% of my money (example: one cent out of every ten cents) 2 1 0
4. I show love to other people mostly by giving them things. 2 1 0
5. I have cheerfully given away good things of mine when I knew someone else needed them more. 2 1 0

ADD IT UP

8

1. I love to help other people by doing physical jobs – cleanup, setup, yard work, hospitality. 2 1 0
2. I would rather work behind the scenes than be up in front of a group. 2 1 0
3. I am a good, responsible worker. 2 1 0
4. I notice when help is needed and jump right in without being asked. 2 1 0
5. If I am getting up to get a drink, I would ask if anyone wanted one (except at school, unless I was at lunch). 2 1 0

ADD IT UP

9

1. I am a good organizer. 2 1 0
2. When things aren't well planned, it drives me crazy. 2 1 0
3. I like to plan my day and organize future events. 2 1 0
4. Once I start something, I am determined to accomplish my goal and am not easily distracted. 2 1 0
5. When people aren't sure what to do, I take charge and get things started. 2 1 0

ADD IT UP

God's Special Gifts For Me

I'm Unique! What's My Gift...

In box "1" below, *(1) Evangelist*, put an X over the number that is equal to your total from box "1" on page 11. Go to box 2 and do the same. Continue until you have completed all 9 boxes. Go back and use a marker to fill-in solid all the numbers to the left of your X. This will form a graph. The highest score shows your strongest gift.

Evangelist = Eagerly tells people about Jesus, persuading them to follow Him.

1 | 1 | 2 | 3 | 4 | 5 | 6 | 7 | 8 | 9 | 10 |

Prophet = Teaches what's wrong and how to change it.

2 | 1 | 2 | 3 | 4 | 5 | 6 | 7 | 8 | 9 | 10 |

Teacher = Plans and researches to teach great lessons.

3 | 1 | 2 | 3 | 4 | 5 | 6 | 7 | 8 | 9 | 10 |

Exhorter = Encourages people to obey and live by God's Word.

4 | 1 | 2 | 3 | 4 | 5 | 6 | 7 | 8 | 9 | 10 |

Shepherd = Looks after the spiritual needs of a group.

5 | 1 | 2 | 3 | 4 | 5 | 6 | 7 | 8 | 9 | 10 |

Mercy Shower = Understands and comforts other people.

6 | 1 | 2 | 3 | 4 | 5 | 6 | 7 | 8 | 9 | 10 |

Giver = Generously shares his or her money and things.

7 | 1 | 2 | 3 | 4 | 5 | 6 | 7 | 8 | 9 | 10 |

Server = Helps other people, does small tasks.

8 | 1 | 2 | 3 | 4 | 5 | 6 | 7 | 8 | 9 | 10 |

Leader = Leads others to accomplish their goals.

9 | 1 | 2 | 3 | 4 | 5 | 6 | 7 | 8 | 9 | 10 |

God's Special Gifts For Me